Literacy, Life Skills, and Character Education
5th Grade Workbook & Journal

Instructor Guide

Supplement to *Life After Birth: A Memoir of Survival and Success as a Teenage Mother* by Summer Owens.

Additional workbooks and books may be ordered through booksellers or by contacting:

Summer Owens

www.SummerOwens.com

ISBN: 978-1-949995-17-6

Printed in the United States of America

Hi there, awesome educator!

I am honored that you are using my real-life story and this workbook with your class, and I believe you'll have a lot of fun and connect with your students on a new level. The S.O. What! Literacy, Life Skills, and Character Education curriculum is a powerful, proven tool designed to facilitate discussion of important topics that affect youth and young adults and aid in educating the student as a whole. Your students will see how I went from being a shy, bullied, and insecure child to a becoming a confident, determined, and successful adult—and how they can apply the lessons I learned to their own lives. Overcoming many obstacles along the way including becoming a teenage mother by someone I did not know, I show students through my journey how to adopt a "S.O. What!" mindset to overcome the challenges in their lives too.

Although academic focused, social and emotional learning concepts as well as Adverse Childhood Experiences (ACEs) awareness are prevalent in each lesson. This in-depth curriculum supports higher learning standards and utilizes the rich resources in Life After Birth. The primary focus is to improve literacy and comprehension by having students examine a text that is relatable, intriguing, and enjoyable for most students. This curriculum combines activities for traditional literacy with analyzing, decision-making, goal-setting and cross-curricular learning to help students learn life skills and develop character. Students will read, watch, research, discuss, and write to educate themselves on topics discussed in the text. Activities included involve peer collaboration, small group, independent learning, and whole group.

The curriculum is flexible and designed for you as the expert in your class to implement as you see most appropriate for your students. Each lesson has several components which you will choose where to focus for the needs of your students. Students should read the designated chapters from *Life After Birth* prior to or during each lesson for optimal engagement. Activities are included for you to follow with class assignments or individual work. Strategies for helping students understand the lesson activities are located before each lesson.

Each lesson has five sections:

- **Vocabulary**
  Students will create "real world" definitions for each vocabulary word identified from the text. "Real world" definitions are created by the student's own vocabulary, using words that they are familiar with to describe something new. These definitions can be fragments or sentences.

- **GROUP TALK**
  Allow students to discuss each of these questions developed from the text content in groups, then have each group answer a question aloud sharing and supporting the details behind their argument.

- **Let's Map it Out**
  Students will create plans, diagrams, plays and more identifying steps for addressing the questions posed based on the reading assignment.

- **RESEARCH MINUTE**
Students will use technology to research information on various topics related to the key ideas identified for each lesson.

- **Quick Facts**
Students will write answers to the questions formed from text content citing evidence from the text to support their answers.

- **Journal**
The journal allows students to reflect on the reading as well as the class discussion and activities and express their feelings based on the journal prompts related to the lesson objectives.

Because of the vast array of topics discussed throughout this curriculum, the primary goals are:

- Improve academic performance, standardized test scores, school attendance rates, graduation rates, and post-secondary attendance rates
- Build digital literacy and STEM skills to support learning in Science, Technology, Engineering, and Math
- Develop college and career goals and workforce readiness
- Develop reading comprehension and writing skills
- Promote literacy, academic excellence, health-related and financial education
- Build self-esteem and help students value themselves and their futures
- Reduce bullying and violence and decrease discipline referrals
- Encourage leadership, teamwork, and community involvement
- Develop character and teach life skills to help students succeed in school and beyond
- Improve emotional learning initiatives
- Reduce teen pregnancy, sexually transmitted disease, poverty, and welfare dependence

Before starting, make your room an environment that is safe for participants to express themselves. Tell all of the participants that the classroom is a safe, confidential environment for them to express themselves openly without ridicule. No one is to put down another for his or her opinions or thoughts. Respect is expected of everyone.

Hope you enjoy using my story and any of your own experiences that you feel comfortable sharing to impact the lives of your students.

Sincerely,

Summer Owens
President and Founder, S.O. What! LLC

Table of Contents

THE S.O. WHAT! STATEMENT

The S.O. What! statement is an empowering and freeing way for students to take away the power from their problems and insecurities. It should be something in their life that bothers them, challenges them, hurts them, or even keeps them from feeling good about themselves or succeeding. The point is to get students to think about situations in their lives or physical characteristics that they may or may not be able to change or do anything about. Often these are the very things that students are picked on about or that keep students from being able to learn or pursue success. Have students write at least one S.O. What! Statement but encourage them to write as many as they would like.

For example:

"S.O. What! I don't know my father."
"S.O. What! I have a bucked teeth."
"S.O. What! I don't have brand name clothes."
"S.O. What! I am short."
"S.O. What! I have parents on drugs."
"S.O. What! I have a disability."

Encourage students to give this statement thought as the act of writing it is a form or release of the hold that the situation or negative feelings the student may be experiencing. Assess your classroom and the students' comfort levels to determine if it is appropriate to share these statements aloud. If the students are mature and willing to share, having the students express their challenges brings commonality and understanding to the group as everyone has issues that affect them and often stifle them. Students who openly share their acceptance of issues that are the cause for bullying take away power from the bullies by demonstrating their own acknowledgment and appreciation for that issue.

For example:

"S.O. What! I have a bucked teeth."

By saying this aloud, any student who tries to bully me with this is met with me saying, "So what. I already know that. I already said that, and I am fine with it."

My S.O. What! Statement

My name is

_____

and

So What

I

_____

The text begins with the foreword by the author explaining that her book is not a celebration of teen pregnancy. Instead, it was written to discourage teen pregnancy yet encourage teen mothers and *everyone* who faces life's challenges. Her story is a testimony that success on all levels is still possible –despite any obstacles one faces.

The introduction exposes a scared Summer giving birth at the young age of 15. She details the experience from the pain and fear to the overwhelming feelings of holding her son for the first time. The story then reverts back to when Summer was a little girl with several insecurities leading to her low-esteem. Students at her school only add to her issues by bullying her. She questions everything about herself including one of the most intricate questions of human's existence, "Who am I?". Use this lesson to help students understand and appreciate themselves as they are and respect others and their differences.

LESSON 1: Discovering *Me*

OBJECTIVE

I will understand how to value myself while respecting others.

KEY IDEAS

- Self-esteem
- Bullying

OTHER TOPICS THAT CAN BE DISCUSSED

- Family structure
- Making a good impression
- Appreciation
- History (Gulf War)

WORDS TO KNOW

Students should provide "real world" definitions" and share with the class.

GROUP TALK

In small groups, have students work together to discover answers to the questions from the text and inject their opinion. Representatives from each group can share the answers from their groups with the class for a larger discussion.

MAP IT OUT!

Replicate Lesson 1 handout by drawing it on the board, placing your name as the topic of discussion. Have students help complete the table with you to discover who you are. Express the importance of being honest and non-judgmental. Let students know that you are creating an environment in which all can grow and learn while beginning to discover who we truly are. Explain that understanding and accepting yourself helps to alleviate bullying, low-esteem, and their negative consequences. For added emphasis, have students look into mirrors as they do this.

RESEARCH IDEA

Using an online resource (computer, ipad, notebook, ipod), research 3 different cultures. Create a table that compares the 3 cultures and you. How are you all similar? in what ways?

JOURNAL

Think about the bullying that Summer experienced. Is your life similar to this or different? How can you impact others positively to prevent bullying?

Discovering *Me*
pp. 1-12

Self-esteem	Bullying

Objective: I will understand how to value myself while respecting others.

Words to Know

After reading aloud, create a "real world" definition for each of the following words with a partner based on context clues from the text. Write your definitions below.

☐ commitment _____
☐ responsibility _____
☐ memorabilia _____
☐ acne _____
☐ reluctant _____
☐ volunteer _____
☐ perseverance _____
☐ commute _____
☐ campus _____

GROUP TALK

Directions: Read the text and discuss the following questions in your group.

1. How was Summer bullied? Why is it not okay to bully others? Explain.

_____

2. Have you ever found yourself following your friends and others by saying negative things to someone just because *they* were doing it? Why is it not okay to join the crowd in bullying or isolating someone else?

_____

3. What could you do to help stop bullying happening to someone else? What are some steps you can take?

_____

4. Did Summer have high self-esteem and take value in herself? Yes or No (Support your answer with sentences from the text.)

_____

☐See What You Know

1. **"I knew I was not pretty or popular, but I didn't understand why basically the entire class proclaimed they hated me."**

   Based on the sentence above, taken from the text on page 3, which of the following is the best synonym for the underlined word?
   A. conversation
   B. shouted
   C. quietly said
   D. silently shouted

2. **"However, it took perseverance to spend my entire summer giving my time away when I wanted to make some money."**

   Based on the sentence above, taken from the text on page 9, which of the following is the best synonym for the underlined word?
   A. spending money
   B. making money
   C. experience
   D. determination

3. In Chapter 1, "The Innocent Little Girl," the author tells us that Summer was called a name she hated, "Stick." Why did her classmates bully her by calling her "Stick"?
   (Use supporting details to support your answer.)

   Answers may vary. They bullied Summer because of her very small size (body).
   Evidence: My clothes barely touched my skinny frame earning me the name, "Stick".

4. Consider all of the things Summer experienced in this text. Was she self-confident and did she have high self-esteem? (Cite evidence from the text to support your argument.)

   Answers may vary. Summer displayed low self-esteem overall; however there were glimpses of self-love coming through. She participated in public things, such as cheerleading.
   Evidence: [1]"I was still very shy and hated how I looked." [2]"I was insecure in so many ways and convinced myself that I was just an ugly girl, …"

5. What negative action showing low self-esteem did Summer do to herself that caused her to have spots in her head? (Use supporting details to support your answer.)

   Answer. She pulled her hair out.
   Evidence: [1] For as long as I could remember, I had been twisting and pulling out my hair and sucking my thumb. [2] With my right hand, I found an area on my head that still had hair and begin twisting it until, eventually; I gave it a nice tug and pulled out a patch of hair creating another little bald spot on my scalp.

"Who am I?"

How do I see myself?	The "Real" Me	How do others see me?

Summer enters high school with many of the insecurities from childhood and some new ones. Dealing with the challenges of the new experience of high school, she finally begins to solidify friendships and even begins to accept herself as she is. However, her desire for acceptance and acknowledgement pushes her to make choices that lead her into a position that creates the biggest change in her future. This part of the book includes sexual intimacy as a result of Summer's insecurities and peer pressure. (No sexual language is used, but the text alludes to what is happening.) A health teacher or representative from the health department could be invited to discuss any details in this lesson around sex education or sexually transmitted diseases.

LESSON 2: The Real Cost of My Decisions

OBJECTIVE

I will learn to make good decisions and prevent problems.

KEY IDEAS

- Decision making
- Avoiding negative situations

OTHER TOPICS THAT CAN BE DISCUSSED

- Attitude
- Judgment
- Volunteering
- Involvement
- Sex

WORDS TO KNOW

Students should provide "real world" definitions" and share with the class.

GROUP TALK

In small groups, have students work together to discover answers to the questions from the text and inject their opinion. Representatives from each group can share the answers from their groups with the class for a larger discussion.

MAP IT OUT!

Using the T-chart in the lesson, have students create a cause and effect list with a partner displaying POSITIVE and NEGATIVE behaviors. Place the actions in the CHOICE (cause) column and the possible results of that action in the CONSEQUENCE (effect) column.

RESEARCH IDEA

Using an online resource (computer, ipad, notebook, ipod), research the common source of problems amongst pre-teens in America. Write an essay comparing the findings to their lives.

JOURNAL

Think about something your parents or teachers have told you to do that you just didn't agree with, so you didn't do it. What were the consequences of your action? Now that you know the end result, what better decision(s) could you have made?

The Real Cost of
My Decisions
pp. 13-33

| Avoiding Negative Situations | Decision-making |

Objective: I will learn to make good decisions and prevent problems.

Words to Know

Based on the context of the reading for this lesson, create a "real world" definition for each of the following words with a partner. Write your definitions below.

- ☐ associate
- ☐ consequence
- ☐ stoic
- ☐ persistent
- ☐ statistic
- ☐ composed
- ☐ clutched
- ☐ disproportionate

GROUP TALK

Directions: Read the text and discuss the following questions in your group.

1. Summer made the decision/choice to try out for cheerleading although she didn't like the way her body looked. What do you think gave her the confidence to try out for cheerleading, knowing that everyone would see her?

2. Using the "Lessons Learned" on page 16, order the main headings (words in **bold** print) from greatest importance to your group to least important. Explain why.

3. Have you ever wanted to be a part of something big and public, such as a cheerleader or an athlete? Were you scared about doing it? How did you overcome your fear and follow through on your decision?

1. Using text from pages 26-27, what was the consequence of Summer going to an empty bedroom at her aunt's house? (Use supporting details to support your answer.)
    A. She got new friends.
    B. She learned how to cook a new dish from her aunt.
    C. **She became pregnant.**
    D. She helped her aunt paint.

2. On page 17, Summer made a public choice concerning her religious faith. Which of the following is similar to this action?
    A. **A Jewish family throwing a Bar Mitzvah (big party) for their teenage son to show that he is becoming a man in God's eyes and has all the rights God allows to a full grown man.**
    B. During the month of Ramadan, Muslims show their devotion to God by fasting, or abstaining from food within the privacy of their homes.
    C. Hinduism is the third largest religion in the world.
    D. An atheist believing to just live life without an acknowledgement of a god.

3. Why do you think Summer chose to have sex? (pp. 19-20) (Use supporting details to support your answer.)

    Answers may vary. Summer's insecurities made her vulnerable to the attention of a boy. She decided it was better to not scream and allow the sexual experience against screaming help or rape.
    Evidence: [1]He rubbed my head, and then touched my stomach, and I cringed as he did, but I didn't make him stop. [2] He proceeded to put his fingers inside of me, and I let him. I guess it was because I was an insecure teenage girl who wanted some attention.   [3]My aunt was asleep, and I didn't want to wake her or draw attention to what was happening so I quietly yelled, "Get off of me," as I struggled to push him away.

4. (p. 23-24) Why was a round-trip bus ticket bought for Summer?
    (Use supporting details to support your answer.)

    Answer. The ticket was bought for Summer to visit her dad for the summer and return home.
    Evidence: A couple of weeks after the incident, my mother bought me a round-trip bus ticket and I headed to Nashville for my regular summer visit to my dad.

5. (pp. 32-33) Other than Summer, who else felt the blame for her pregnancy?
    (Use supporting details to support your answer.)
    Answers may vary. Summer's aunt Pat
    Evidence: ... I just really hate this whole situation. It's my fault. I'm so sorry, Summer."

MAP IT OUT!

Using the T-chart below, create a cause and effect list with your partner of POSITIVE and NEGATIVE behaviors. Place the action in the CHOICE (cause) column and the possible result of that action in the CONSEQUENCE (effect) column.

CHOICE (cause)	CONSEQUENCE (effect)

Summer experiences feelings of disbelief due to now being pregnant at 15. The effects of her pregnancy on her emotionally, as she considers and threatens suicide, and physically as her body begins to change really challenge her spirit. Her need for support is evident and appreciated as her mother, and the entire school, finds out about her pregnancy. She begins to accept her new situation and to think about her future. Use this lesson to help students think about the change that happens in their lives as a result of choices they make and to focus on methods of dealing with that change.

LESSON 3: How to Deal with Change

OBJECTIVE

I will accept internal and external changes as I grow.

KEY IDEAS

- Cause and Effect
- Teen Pregnancy
- Emotions

OTHER TOPICS THAT CAN BE DISCUSSED

- Government support/dependence
- Boyfriend/Girlfriend relationships
- Travel
- Communication

WORDS TO KNOW

Students should provide "real world" definitions" and share with the class.

GROUP TALK

In small groups, have students work together to discover answers to the questions from the text and inject their opinion. Representatives from each group can share the answers from their groups with the class for a larger discussion.

MAP IT OUT & SUMMARIZE!

Have students try to infer their responses if they were expecting a baby. Fill in the boxes to show the main changes that Summer experienced after finding out she was pregnant.

RESEARCH IDEA

Using an online resource (computer, ipad, notebook, ipod), research the stages of human development and how physical & biological changes can affect how one sees him/herself.

JOURNAL

Think about what it is like to be the most popular kid in school. Think about what it is like for those who are quiet and shy, unnoticed. Write a letter to a new student and tell them how to navigate going through a new school, how should they adapt to their new environment (making new friends, staying away from the wrong group, being a part of something positive, …)

How to Deal with Change
pp. 34-47

| Teen pregnancy | Emotions | Cause & Effect |

Objective: I will accept internal and external changes as I grow.

Words to Know

Based on the context of the reading for this lesson, create a "real world" definition for each of the following words with a partner. Write your definitions below.

- ☐ challenge
- ☐ emotions
- ☐ abortion
- ☐ perseverance
- ☐ consequence
- ☐ rejection

GROUP TALK

Directions: Read the text and discuss the following questions in your group.

1. What big change is causing Summer the biggest challenge of her young life?

2. What big change have you experienced this school year? How are you dealing with it or how did you deal with it?

3. Why did Summer want to take her own life?

4. What are some things a person can do if they become overwhelmed and want to let go of their life (suicide)? Who can they talk to?

5. On page 46, Summer said she was experiencing a mix of emotions. What do you think she was feeling? Why is it completely normal to feel different emotions in life?

1. Which of the following quotes from the text (p. 38) does **not** support the idea that Summer believes Markus can be the father of her unborn baby?
   A. "Summer, I know. I already heard, but you know it's not mine."
   B. "Markus, I think it is. You know I'm not sure that it really happened with him, but I know it did with you."
   C. **"…, it was official that I was going to be a mother before my sixteenth birthday."**
   D. "As he shook his head reiterating that he knew the baby growing inside of me was not his, …"

2. **(p. 42) As the weeks went by and I began to accept the *inevitable truth* that I was going to be a teenage mother, my mother set my first doctor's appointment.**

   Which of the following can you conclude from this statement?
   A. Summer is going to give her baby up for adoption.
   B. Summer is having twins.
   C. Summer hates doctor's appointments.
   D. **Summer has accepted the fact that she is going to be a mother.**

3. (p. 37) What evidence supports the fact that Summer was ashamed to become a teenage mother? (Use supporting details to support your answer.)
   Answers may vary.
   Evidence: [1] Lying on the bottom bunk of the set I had shared with Brandy for my entire life, I cried and wished that I could just die so that I would not have to live with the embarrassment of the pregnancy and endure the hard life that would follow.
   [2] It was still very difficult to fathom being pregnant by someone I didn't know, …

4. According to the text on page 44, what was the purpose of Women, Infants, and Children (WIC)? (Use supporting details to support your answer.)
   Answer. a means to support both mom and baby with nutritious foods
   Evidence: A form of public assistance, the WIC program was designed to help ensure pregnant mothers had access to nutritious food for themselves and their unborn babies.

MAP IT OUT & SUMMARIZE!

Fill in the boxes below to show the main changes that Summer experienced after finding out she was pregnant.

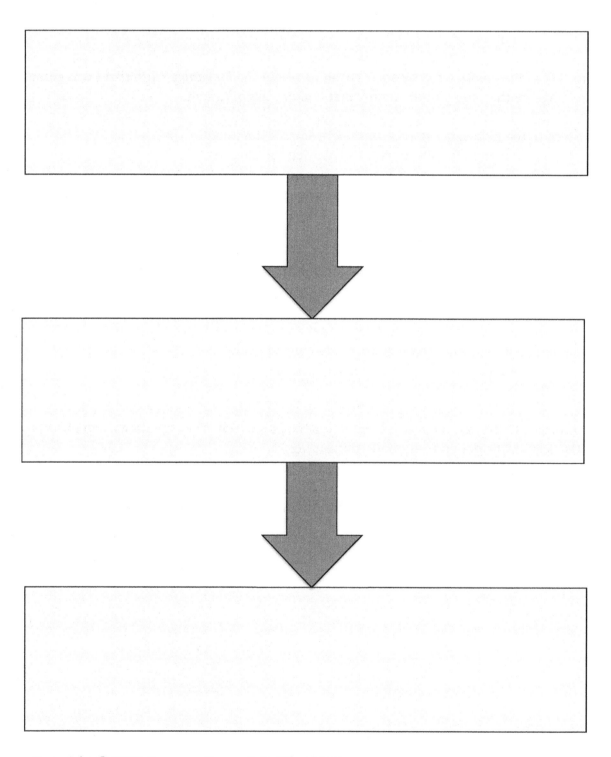

Summer begins to see the true importance of having support in your life, like her family and true friends. The moment she had been fearing from the time she found out that she was pregnant arrived—she gave birth and the reality that having babies as a child was not easy really set in. She accepted her new reality and decided to make the most of it despite her fears but still wondered if the boy who forced himself on her or her former boyfriend was the father of her baby. Use this lesson to emphasize the impact of friends both positively and negatively. Also, point out how Summer viewed money and materialism.

LESSON 4: Who Cares What *They* Say?

OBJECTIVE

I will understand how my friends can influence me to do right or wrong.

KEY IDEAS

- Positive/negative influences

OTHER TOPICS THAT CAN BE DISCUSSED

- Courage
- Taking pride in your work

WORDS TO KNOW

Students should provide "real world" definitions" and share with the class.

GROUP TALK

In small groups, have students work together to discover answers to the questions from the text and inject their opinion. Representatives from each group can share the answers from their groups with the class for a larger discussion.

RESEARCH IDEA

Research ways for kids to save and make money. Make a list and circle the things you could do now.

JOURNAL

Think about how you believe kids would feel if they are very depressed or bullied. Write a letter to that student, expressing how they can deal with their situation and not do anything to hurt themselves or others.

Who Cares What *They* Say?

pp. 48-66

Positive/Negative Influences	Savings

Objective: I will understand how my friends can influence me to do right or wrong.

Words to Know

Based on the context of the reading for this lesson, create a "real world" definition for each of the following words with a partner. Write your definitions below.

- influence _____
- friendship _____
- support _____
- peer pressure _____
- savings _____
- judging _____

GROUP TALK

Directions: Read the text and discuss the following questions in your group.

1. Summer had friends that accepted her in her pregnant state. Do you think they should have accepted her since she was becoming a teen mother? Why or why not?
   _____

2. Why is it important to be nice to people, even if they have made a mistake?
   _____

3. What were some ways Summer's family and friends positively influenced her?
   _____
   _____

4. What are some things you can do when people say negative things about you?
   _____
   _____

1. "Being a <u>stubborn</u> child, I had never had the best relationship with my stepfather. "

   Consider the context of this sentence taken from page 49, which of the following behaviors support the author's description of Summer as being a <u>stubborn</u> child?
   A. We played a few games, ate, and then, "Open your gifts!" the room later excitedly expressed sounding even more anxious to see the gifts than I was.
   B. Because I hadn't ironed my clothes yet, I refused.
   C. With only the clothes on my back, I stormed out of the house without a destination at first.
   D. Not noticing when I left, my stepfather didn't know I was gone and my mother still hadn't returned.

2. "....., I almost didn't feel the pressure of the knife as the doctor began to cut through the layers of my abdomen." (p.56)

   Considering all that was happening with Summer in this section of the story, what part of her body was receiving a surgical incision, as stated in the quote above?
   A. her arms
   B. her stomach
   C. her legs
   D. her head

3. Based on page 48, how does the author show us that Summer was cared about?
   (Use supporting details to support your answer.)
   Suggestion: **Ask the students to find two sentences that support this question.**
   Evidence: [1] I had a great group of friends who supported me throughout my entire pregnancy.
   [2] ..., I usually had someone to talk to or cry with when I was down.
   [3] Sitting there I beamed as I scanned the room full of people who cared about me.
   [4] I couldn't believe my friends were having a baby shower for me because we were all still broke little girls.

4. Identify details to support Summer and her mother's positive relationship, despite the situation.
   (Use supporting details to support your answer.)
   Answers may vary.
   Evidence: [1] My mother had endured three C-sections, and I was thankful she was there to comfort me; but I was still scared.
   [2] For a very short period of time, she rubbed my head and said all she knew to say, "Well, Summer. It will be okay. It'll be over before you know it."

Summer is still uncertain about who the father of her baby is but finally is able to take a blood test but must wait on the results. In the meantime, she also realizes how expensive it is to take care of a baby and herself. She takes big steps in growing up and demonstrating responsibility by getting her first official job and her first car. This lesson allows students to see the effects of drastic changes in life and how to cope.

LESSON 5: Accepting Responsibility

OBJECTIVE

I will take responsibility for myself and my future.

KEY IDEAS

- Responsibility
- Goal-setting
- Handling disappointment

OTHER TOPICS THAT CAN BE DISCUSSED

- Time Management
- Self-motivation

WORDS TO KNOW

Students should provide "real world" definitions" and share with the class.

GROUP TALK

In small groups, have students work together to discover answers to the questions from the text and inject their opinion. Representatives from each group can share the answers from their groups with the class for a larger discussion.

MAP IT OUT!

With a peer, have students make a table showing 3 things they can do to take responsibility for their own individual actions *now* and in the future, even if it's different from their friends.

RESEARCH IDEA

Students research the road taken by their favorite celebrity to get to the top. How did they start out? What things did they go through? Create a timeline showing the steps that led to their goal of becoming_____.

JOURNAL

Why is it important to take responsibility for your own actions and choices? How does talking to an adult before you make a big decision affect your outcomes?

Accepting Responsibility
pp. 67-75

| Goal-setting | Responsibility | Handling Disappointment |

Objective: I will take responsibility for myself and my future.

Words to Know

Based on the context of the reading for this lesson, create a "real world" definition for each of the following words with a partner. Write your definitions below.

- ☐ responsibility
- ☐ goals
- ☐ transportation
- ☐ car note
- ☐ routine
- ☐ decision

GROUP TALK

Directions: Read the text and discuss the following questions in your group.

1. How did the results of the paternity test disappoint Summer? Explain.
   _____

2. How do you handle disappointment when you've been really hoping for something that didn't come true? Explain.
   _____

3. What goal (plan) did Summer come up with to make money? (Support your answer with sentences from the text.)
   _____

4. What are some goals that you can set for yourself to become a better student at school and a better kid to your parents at home?
   _____

√ **SEE WHAT YOU KNOW**   **LESSON 5**

1. Which of the following statements from the story support Summer showing responsibility?
   A. **…, I filled out the application and was hired on the spot, received my shirt and cap, and started working two days later.**
   B. Catching a ride to school was no problem because they were going to the same place.
   C. My grandmother couldn't drive and did not own a vehicle.
   D. I wanted to one day be able to have anything and go anywhere I wanted rather than waiting on food stamps or a check to pay my bills.

2. **"I usually worked about fifteen hours each week and was typically on the schedule starting at 5:00 or 6:00 PM …"**

   Based on the statement above, what are the two possible times Summer likely got off work if she worked five days a week?
   A. 6:00PM or 7:00PM
   B. 7:00PM or 8:00PM
   C. **8:00PM or 9:00PM**
   D. 10:00PM or 11:00PM

3. (pp. 73-74) How do we know Summer managed her time well?
   (Use supporting details to support your answer.)
   Answers may vary. Her day was filled with times to be at various places starting from going to school in the mornings to making it to work on time each day.
   Evidence: I usually worked about fifteen hours each week and was typically on the schedule starting at 5:00 or 6:00 PM so my routine was to come home from school around 3:00 PM on days when I did not have any afterschool meetings or activities. Once I got home from school, I relieved my grandmother of her babysitting duties and brought my baby to my bedroom or the living room and placed him in his swing, walker, playpen or carrier and started on my homework.

4. (p. 70) What responsibility did Summer have to deal with in her future that Markus did not?
   (Use supporting details to support your answer.)
   Answers may vary. She would be a teen parent.
   Evidence: It stated that with 99.7% certainty, Markus was not my son's father.

5. (pp. 73-74) What are some ways that the author shows us that Summer motivated herself to do positive things and stay on the right track? (Use supporting details to support your answer.)
   Answers may vary. She figured out a way to get a car; she created a schedule that allotted her to be independent, while making time for her son. She listened to positive music.
   Evidence: Driving home from work in my little white Neon, I played what was still my favorite cassette, "I Will Survive" constantly fighting to stay encouraged through my situation and also to help me stay awake after the long days at school and work. Once he calmed down, I began my attempt to put him to sleep so that I could finish my homework that I usually never was able to finish before going to work.

MAP IT OUT!

With a peer, make a table showing 3 things that you can do to take responsibility now for your actions and future, even if your friends don't do it. Share.

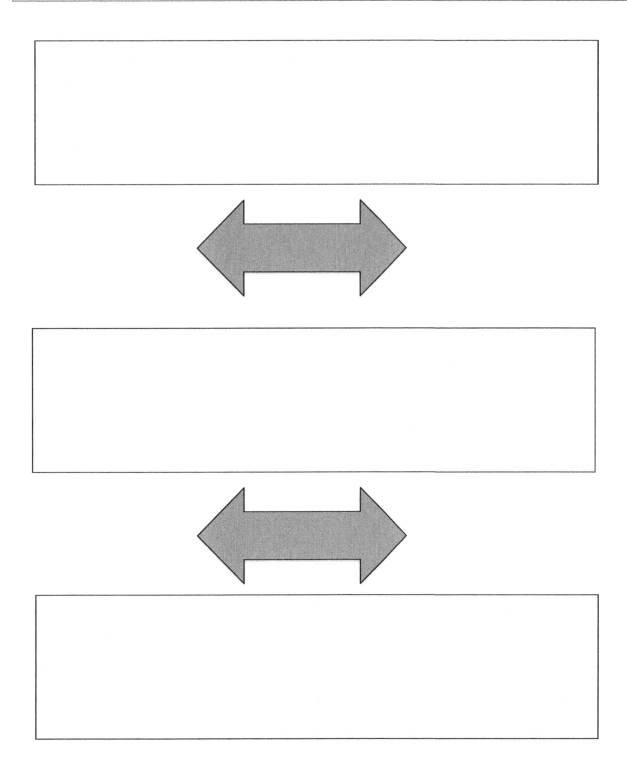

Summer reaches the end of her high school experience. She still struggles with some insecurities but is selected for some opportunities that help her self-confidence. Graduating in the top 10 of her class, she receives a scholarship to the University of Memphis and makes the difficult decision to move away from her son. Use this lesson to help students realize the value of hard work to overcome obstacles and mistakes that may set them back. College preparation and the importance of college should also be a focus for this lesson.

LESSON 6: "I Made a Mistake, Now What?"

OBJECTIVE

I will encourage myself, even after I have made mistakes.

KEY IDEAS

- Thinking Ahead
- Communication

OTHER TOPICS THAT CAN BE DISCUSSED

- Scholarships
- Financial Aid
- Perseverance
- Self-motivation

WORDS TO KNOW

Students should provide "real world" definitions" and share with the class.

GROUP TALK

In small groups, have students work together to discover answers to the questions from the text and inject their opinion. Representatives from each group can share the answers from their groups with the class for a larger discussion.

RESEARCH IDEA

Students research the life of Martin Luther King, Jr. or Gandhi. How were they encouraged to do what they did when so many were against them? How did they communicate in the midst of the threats and hatred? Why is this important for your life now?

JOURNAL

Explain why it's important to plan ahead now in school for your future college years?

I Made a Mistake, Now What?

pp. 76-87

Thinking Ahead	Communication

Objective: I will encourage myself, even after I have made mistakes.

Words to Know

Based on the context of the reading for this lesson, create a "real world" definition for each of the following words with a partner. Write your definitions below.

- ☐ Frosh
- ☐ commitment
- ☐ obstacles
- ☐ extracurricular
- ☐ disproportionate
- ☐ commencement
- ☐ scholarship
- ☐ leadership

GROUP TALK

Directions: Read the text and discuss the following questions in your group.

1. How did being a good student in high school help Summer beyond her mistake? Explain.

2. What are some ways you can change a mistake and replace it with a positive action? Explain.

3. In what way did the positive effects of Summer doing well in school affect her ability to go to college? (Support your answer with sentences from the text.)

4. What is the relationship between good grades and scholarships?

1. "My family supported me because they saw my <u>commitment</u> and my effort to being a good mother. <u>Commitment</u> and effort were very much needed in every aspect of my life especially with raising Jaylan."

    Based on the sentences above, which of the following words is a synonym for "commitment"?
       A. carelessness
       B. thoughtfulness
       C. dedication
       D. irresponsibility

2. (p. 81) Because of miscommunication by the school's counselor, Summer was disappointed at her high school graduation. What did the miscommunication cause?
       A. Summer to be nominated in the top ten of her class
       B. Summer to go on stage with her son Jaylan
       C. Summer to walk on the crosswalk
       D. Summer's scholarship not to be announced

3. (pp. 76-77) Summer realized she could not afford pampers or pull-ups, what steps did she take to plan ahead to alleviate (lessen) that burden? (Cite evidence from the text to support your argument.)
    Answers may vary. She potty-trained her son.
    Evidence: Because pampers and eventually pull-ups were such a burden on my limited budget, I began my efforts to potty train as soon as he tried to walk.

4. (p. 79) Identify supporting details that show that Summer had good communication skills. (Use supporting details to support your answer.)
    Answers may vary. Summer exhibited a large vocabulary and was able to describe things easily.
    Evidence: Mine was a metallic lavender material made from three different dress patterns,… awning our new dresses, clear Cinderella slippers, makeup and fancy pinned up hair do's, we were ready to go.

5. (p. 79) Even with continuous communication with others, why does Summer still feel alone? (Cite evidence from the text to support your argument.)
    Answers may vary. She feels like she is the only one that can identify with what she is experiencing.
    Evidence: Most days, I cried and felt sorry for myself because no one understood what I was going through or how I felt. No one could help me on the inside, and sometimes no one could help on the outside either.

Summer is learning how to adapt to the new environment of college life and how to manage her time and financial obligations. Although she lives in another city, she remains connected to her son even bringing him to campus with her. Her determination and priorities are challenged as she also deals with the responsibilities of motherhood. Use this lesson to demonstrate the importance of sacrifice and setting priorities for long-term benefit.

LESSON 7: "College Life"

OBJECTIVE

I will adapt when change comes.

KEY IDEAS

- Adapting to change
- Sacrifice
- Financial responsibility

OTHER TOPICS THAT CAN BE DISCUSSED

- Resourcefulness / Time-management
- Determination /Leadership /Prioritizing
- Asking for & appreciating help

WORDS TO KNOW

Students should provide "real world" definitions" and share with the class.

GROUP TALK

In small groups, have students work together to discover answers to the questions from the text and inject their opinion. Representatives from each group can share the answers from their groups with the class for a larger discussion.

RESEARCH IDEA

Referencing the research done on Martin Luther King, Jr. or Grande, compare Summer and the person you chose. What are some ways they were alike?

JOURNAL

What can you do to adapt to a new environment and what can you do to help someone else?

College Life
pp. 88-102

| Adapting to Change | Sacrifice | Financial Responsibility |

Objective: I will adapt when change comes.

Words to Know

Based on the context of the reading for this lesson, create a "real world" definition for each of the following words with a partner. Write your definitions below.

☐ environment _____

☐ sacrifice _____

☐ adapting _____

☐ anxiety _____

☐ dorm _____

☐ sorority _____

☐ intern _____

GROUP TALK

Directions: Read the text and discuss the following questions in your group.

1. What sacrifice did Summer have to make in order to move on campus to go to college? (Support your answer with sentences from the text.)

   _____

2. What was the purpose of Summer making that sacrifice?

   _____

3. What kind of sacrifices could you make that would make school or home life better for you?

   _____

4. What were some changes Summer experienced living on campus?

   _____

   _____

1. "Pulling into the parking lot of my <u>dorm</u>, we saw hundreds of other students were moving in too. We first unloaded the big items on the back of my dad's truck and headed inside. I had gotten my room assignment earlier and knew that my room was on the 7th floor."

   Based on the insert above, which of these is most closely related to the meaning of the word, "dorm"? (Use supporting details to support your answer.)
   - **A. student housing**
   - B. grandma's house
   - C. childhood housing
   - D. college classes

2. Because Summer could not see her son very much due to school and work, she sacrificed _____the most with her son.
   - A. housing
   - **B. time**
   - C. classes
   - D. school

3. (p. 92) What are some ways Summer proved to be financially responsible?
   (Cite evidence from the text to support your argument.)
   Answer. She paid for a college course in summer school, helped her grandmother, paid her car note, and saved money.
   Evidence: Back home for the summer, I enrolled in a history class at the local community college to get a few credits out of the way while I was at home. I also got a job at a shoe store to pay for the course, to help out my grandmother, to pay my car note and to put aside money for the upcoming semester.

4. (p. 101) Summer needed government assistance through the form of food stamps and welfare. She finally got the courage to apply. What were the results? (Use supporting details to support your answer.)
   Answers may vary. She was denied both food stamps and welfare.
   Evidence: Looking for other forms of income, I applied for public assistance and attempted to secure child support. Many college students I knew received food stamps, and I knew that if I could get food stamps then I could use the money I spent on food to pay my bills. However, I was told that I did not qualify because I had a car in my name.

5. Based on question 4, do you think the state (department of human services) maybe made the right decision with Summer? Explain. What lesson did Summer learn from being denied assistance?
   Answers may vary. Having a car in one's name doesn't mean she is able to support herself with a child. It doesn't seem logical to help single college students with no children that live in the same condition as a mother with a child. She learned that she could survive without public assistance and learned to work harder and manage her money even better.

Summer's son begins school as Summer earns her bachelor's degree. She deals with the stress of being a full-time, single mother and an active student leader. Three unexpected honors reassure Summer that her hard work is paying off. Use this lesson to share the importance of setting goals in education and how discipline helps one accomplish their goals and aspirations.

LESSON 8: "Reaching Our Goals"

OBJECTIVE

I will learn the importance of creating goals/plans.

KEY IDEAS

- Discipline
- Importance of Education
- Accomplishments

OTHER TOPICS THAT CAN BE DISCUSSED

- Goal-setting
- Time-management
- Graduation
- College

WORDS TO KNOW

Students should provide "real world" definitions" and share with the class.

GROUP TALK

In small groups, have students work together to discover answers to the questions from the text and inject their opinion. Representatives from each group can share the answers from their groups with the class for a larger discussion.

MAP IT OUT!

Have students make a list of goals based on the time it takes to do them using the Short-Term and Long-Term table. Review the examples with them.

RESEARCH IDEA

Students research ways to obtain their long-term goals placed on the table.

JOURNAL

Think of something you really want right now (join an athletic team, learn to type, make better grades, …). How can you achieve that goal? What are some things you need to do in order to accomplish your goal?

Reaching Our Goals
pp. 103-115

| Discipline | Importance of Education | Accomplishments |

Objective: I will learn the importance of creating goals/plans.

Words to Know

Based on the context of the reading for this lesson, create a "real world" definition for each of the following words with a partner. Write your definitions below.

☐ goals

☐ discipline

☐ accomplishment

☐ requirements

☐ stress

☐ focus

GROUP TALK

Directions: Read the text and discuss the following questions in your group.

1. What are some ways the author shows us that Summer was disciplined and determined, even though at times she wanted to give up?

2. What can you do when school is hard and you want to give up? Why is it important to persevere and get an education?

3. How did gaining a college degree help Summer? What was the importance of her getting that level of education?

4. How can you discipline yourself and stay focused on school, so you are able to graduate and attend college when your friends are trying to get you get off task?
(Support your answer with sentences from the text.)

1. Which supporting sentence from the text shows that education was important both for Summer and her son?
    A. …,I found some relief when Jaylan visited her and played games with her and her boyfriend while I did homework.
    B. I stayed up late almost every night doing homework and completing the requirements for my bachelor's degree.
    C. When I got stressed out with homework or with being a mother for all the various reasons as I often did, I pictured how much easier my life would be if it were normal.
    D. When he made it inside, we did his homework together then I let him play outside while I started my own homework.

2. If Summer became friends with Chinitra at age 8 and graduated at 22, how long had she been a friend to Chinitra when she graduated college?
    A. 22 years
    B. 20 years
    C. 15 years
    D. 14 years

3. (pp. 108-110) What are 2 accomplishments that Summer achieved in college?
    (Use supporting details to support your answer.)
    Answers. Summer's accomplishments in college: Sorority Recognition for significant contributions, Marketing Major of the Year, Miss University of Memphis
    Evidence: …, my chapter had chosen me to receive the award for the college student who had made significant contributions to the campus and to the community. … selected as the business school's undergraduate marketing management major of the year. In fact, it was the most prestigious award any female student could receive, Miss University of Memphis.

4. What are some things in the text that shows Summer managed her time well? (Use supporting details to support your answer.)
    Answers may vary. She made sure she and her son had a routine to do homework, eat dinner, and be at their schools on time.
    Evidence: I set my class schedule according to Jaylan's school schedule so that I was in school when he was and back home before him, and I worked a few hours on my internship in between classes. In the afternoon, I watched from my balcony for the boys to head back towards the apartment. When he made it inside, we did his homework together then I let him play outside while I started my own homework.

5. (p. 103) What step taken by Summer shows her fulfilling a goal set for her son? (Use supporting details to support your answer.)
    Answers may vary. She celebrated his 5th birthday through a party with family and friends.
    Evidence: A handful of kids and more adults, my mother, grandmother and friends, participated in the momentous occasion. With my tiny budget, I created the best hot dogs, chips, cake and ice cream he had ever had.

MAP IT OUT!
Make a list of your goals based on the time it takes to do them.
Short-term: 2 months or less   **Long-term: over 2 months**

"Short-term and Long-term Goals"

Short-term Goals (2 months or less)	Long-term Goals (over 2 months)
Score an A on my English test next week	Make the honor roll at the end of the semester.

LESSON 9: "Time to Work"

OBJECTIVE

I will understand the relationship between hard work and a good future.

KEY IDEAS

- Good impression
- Persistence

OTHER TOPICS THAT CAN BE DISCUSSED

- Creativity
- Punctual
- Sacrifice
- Goals

WORDS TO KNOW

Students should provide "real world" definitions" and share with the class.

GROUP TALK

In small groups, have students work together to discover answers to the questions from the text and inject their opinion. Representatives from each group can share the answers from their groups with the class for a larger discussion.

MAP IT OUT!

This is a great visual activity for students to see the importance of schooling at every step in order to have a career.

RESEARCH IDEA

POWERPOINT:
Create a PowerPoint highlighting the path to each step from Elementary to Career. Use "Ladder to Career" organizer as a guide.

JOURNAL

Write down some positives you've identified in a recent negative situation you've experienced. What did you learn from this experience?

Armed with a college degree, Summer begins her hunt for a job and life in the "real world." She unexpectedly has a difficult time getting interviews and her first job but eventually earns her first job and several lessons along the way. The work she had done in college by being involved in campus organizations was showing benefits.

Time to Work
pp. 116-130

Good Impression	Hard Work

Objective: I will understand the relationship between hard work and a good future.

Words to Know

Based on the context of the reading for this lesson, create a "real world" definition for each of the following words with a partner. Write your definitions below.

- ☐ presentable
- ☐ impression
- ☐ internship
- ☐ persistent
- ☐ inquisitive

GROUP TALK

Directions: Read the text and discuss the following questions in your group.

1. How did persistence play a role in Summer staying in high school, then college, despite being a teenage mother?

2. What are some things you can do to keep your focus when you don't like a teacher or student in your room?

3. Identify some ways Summer presented herself in interviews. Be very specific.

4. Why is it important to look your best and act your best all of the time? How does that affect the way the adults that teach you see you?

1. Based on the text of page 117, why was Summer considering moving back to Jackson to live with her grandmother?
    - **A. She couldn't find a job.**
    - B. She missed her grandmother so much.
    - C. Jaylan didn't like Memphis.
    - D. She and her friend Chinitra had a big fight.

2. (pp. 117-118) What was the positive reason Summer chose to accept the job at the rental car company?
    - A. It offered large bonuses.
    - B. It was closer to Jackson.
    - **C. It offered health insurance and more money.**
    - D. It offered health insurance and a signing bonus.

3. (p. 116) What did Summer learn from being an intern at the hotel?
    (Use supporting details to support your answer.)
    Answers may vary. She learned she did not like sales.
    Evidence: I learned a lot from the experience, but one of the main things I learned was that I did not want to work in sales. I only wanted to work in marketing.

4. By waiting two days to give an answer to an offer from the rental car company, what disappointment did Summer incur? (Use supporting details to support your answer.)
    Answers may vary. She lost the job. They had chosen someone else while she considered.
    Evidence: He asked me to let you know that we've decided to pursue other candidates."

5. (p. 118) What choice did Summer make to continue her education? What were the reasons she chose to do this? (Use supporting details to support your answer.)
    Answers may vary. She decided to go to graduate school after she was unsuccessful in securing a job.
    Evidence: I really didn't want to move back home though. Still pondering other options, I decided to go back to school and pursue my MBA since I knew I eventually wanted to earn it anyway.

<table>
<tr><td>MAP IT OUT
Think back to Summer's journey that led her to her career (job). Create a PowerPoint highlighting the path to each step from Elementary to Career.</td></tr>
</table>

"Ladder to Career"

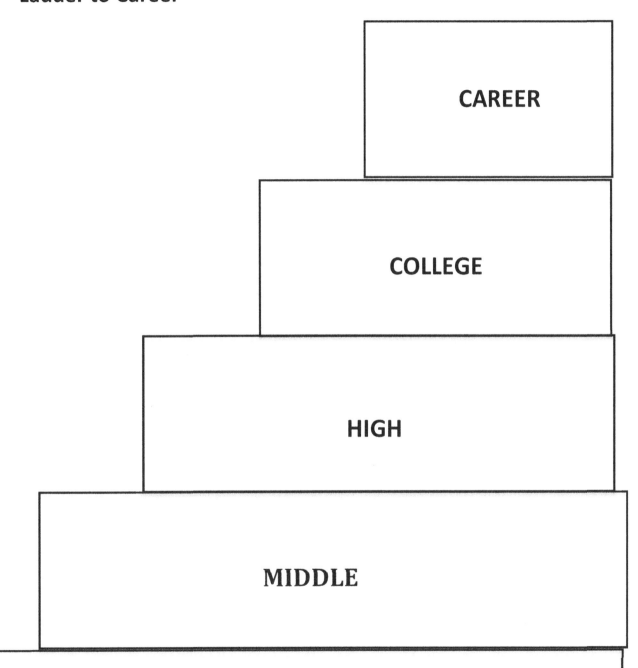

CAREER

COLLEGE

HIGH

MIDDLE

ELEMENTARY

Summer gets settled into her position, and although her salary is much less than she expected it would be as a college graduate with her background, she decides to buy a house for her and her son. She uses various creative techniques to save the limited money she has to support her family and achieve what some people thought was impossible for her. Use this lesson to show students the importance of understanding money and finances, setting financial goals, and making sacrifices to achieve financially smart goals. Reference previous chapters where Summer demonstrated her financial priorities even in high school. Using Handout 9, guide students through a simple budget. A link to budget spreadsheets is included in the lesson plan.

LESSON 10: "Money"

OBJECTIVE

I will learn the importance of saving.

KEY IDEAS

- Savings
- Patience

OTHER TOPICS THAT CAN BE DISCUSSED

- Prioritizing
- Budgeting

WORDS TO KNOW

Students should provide "real world" definitions" and share with the class.

GROUP TALK

In small groups, have students work together to discover answers to the questions from the text and inject their opinion. Representatives from each group can share the answers from their groups with the class for a larger discussion.

RESEARCH IDEA⬜⬜

The purpose of this activity is for you to get a "real world" perspective on the dollar amount for real jobs. Go to the following site to see the top paying jobs in our country. Make a list of the 5 you may be interested in doing as an adult.
http://www.glassdoor.com/blog/highest-paying-jobs-demand/

JOURNAL

Based on your reading and discussions, explain why it is important to save today for tomorrow.

Money
pp. 130-138

| Savings | | Patience |

Objective: I will learn the importance of saving.

Words to Know

Based on the context of the reading for this lesson, create a "real world" definition for each of the following words with a partner. Write your definitions below.

☐ budget _____

☐ savings _____

☐ patience _____

☐ sacrifice _____

GROUP TALK

Directions: Read the text and discuss the following questions in your group.

1. What are some ways Summer saved money?

   _____

   _____

2. Is there anything you can save? If so, how can you save it?

   _____

   _____

3. What are the things Summer spent money on? What are some things she did not?

   _____

   _____

4. Why was it important for Summer to be patient and disciplined with her money, instead of going out and purchasing the latest iPhone or game system?
   (Support your answer with sentences from the text.)

   _____

   _____

1. Based on the reading in pages 130-131, what was the benefit of using a credit union?
    - **A.** It gave extra money to people who were nice.
    - **B.** **It made it difficult for Summer to get money out of the bank, which helped with saving.**
    - **C.** It had branches that were close to her to help her save.
    - **D.** Every paycheck came from them.

2. (pp. 130-131) Which of the following was not a responsibility Summer had?
    - **A.** **Pay mortgage insurance**
    - **B.** Pay a car note
    - **C.** Pay a utility bill
    - **D.** Pay rent

3. (p. 132) What did Summer eliminate to cause her income to go further?
    (Use the text to support your answer.)
    Answers may vary. Summer stopped getting her hair done at a salon.
    Evidence: Regular hair appointments which were already infrequent were eliminated.

4. (p. 130) What steps did Summer take to ensure she would start saving for her future?
    (Use the text to support your answer.)
    Answers may vary. She opened up an account at a credit union and set an automatic deposit from her job.
    Evidence: As soon as I was hired into the marketing department, I set up a savings account at a credit union with an automatic deposit of $100 from every paycheck.

RESEARCH MINUTE

The purpose of this activity is for you to get a "real world" perspective on the dollar amount for real jobs. Go to the following site to see the top paying jobs in our country. Make a list of the top 10. http://www.glassdoor.com/blog/highest-paying-jobs-demand/

JOB	YEARLY SALARY

Copyright © 2021 Summer Owens S.O. What! LLC

Balancing her life as a single mother and employee at a job where she worked well over 40 hours each week, Summer adds the title of full-time student when she decides to pursue her MBA. The stress and pressure increase, but she is determined to position herself to earn more money and have even more options for career.

LESSON 11: "Today *Builds* Tomorrow"

OBJECTIVE

I will learn to make and follow a schedule to accomplish things in my life.

KEY IDEAS

- Integrity
- Teamwork
- Dependability

OTHER TOPICS THAT CAN BE DISCUSSED

- Progression
- Time-management
- Value of education
- Procrastination

WORDS TO KNOW

Students should provide "real world" definitions" and share with the class.

GROUP TALK

In small groups, have students work together to discover answers to the questions from the text and inject their opinion. Representatives from each group can share the answers from their groups with the class for a larger discussion.

MAP IT OUT!

With a neighbor, have students create a schedule that students could use for school a day. (If time permits, include the weekend.) Include: wake-up time, breakfast, your class schedule, homework time, reading time, dinner, bedtime.

RESEARCH MINUTE

Research different templates for a schedule. Choose one that would fit your life.

JOURNAL

In a paragraph or two, explain the importance of teamwork in achieving one common goal.

Today *Builds* Tomorrow
pp. 139-152

Integrity	Teamwork	Dependability

Objective: I will learn to make and follow a schedule to accomplish things in my life.

Words to Know

Based on the context of the reading for this lesson, create a "real world" definition for each of the following words with a partner. Write your definitions below.

☐ time management _____

☐ teamwork _____

☐ dependable _____

☐ promotion _____

☐ integrity _____

☐ pursue _____

GROUP TALK

Directions: Read the text and discuss the following questions in your group.

1. Why was it necessary for each person on Summer's marketing team at work to depend on each other to do their part? How does this help the whole project their working on?

   _____
   _____

2. When you're working in a group in your classroom, how can each person in the group contribute toward getting the task done assigned by your teacher?

   _____
   _____

3. What were some ways Summer demonstrated integrity on her job?

   _____
   _____

4. Why is it important for every student to walk with integrity? What's the point?

   _____
   _____

1. (pp. 139-141) What was the main obstacle in preventing Summer from possibly attending Grizzlies games for her job on Thursdays?
   - **A. going to school**
   - B. being a full-time mother
   - C. not enough tickets to the game
   - D. Jaylan's practice

2. (p. 143) What scheduled routine did Summer do with her son to prepare for the week?
   - A. homework for the week
   - **B. selecting and ironing Jaylan's clothes for the week**
   - C. writing a check
   - D. talk about homework

3. What did Summer do to make time for herself each day? (Use supporting details to support your answer.)
   Answers may vary. She had Jaylan go to bed at 8:30p.m.
   Evidence: His bedtime was 8:30 PM, and that was both for him and for me. He was a young child and needed to go to bed at a reasonable time, and I needed time for myself.

4. In the "Lesson Learned" on page 145, what did the author mean by finding "a more efficient use of my time"? (Use supporting details to support your answer.)
   Answers may vary slightly. She was stating the need to use her time wisely.

My Daily Schedule

Summer continues working long hours and feels a sense of guilt for her time away from her son, but she finds ways to incorporate her son into her career and make it fun for him. She also exposes her son to traveling to new places and having new experiences. Use this lesson to introduce students to being open to traveling, exploring new places, and having new experiences beyond their comfort zones.

LESSON 12: "Disappointments"

OBJECTIVE

I will not let disappointments cause me to quit.

KEY IDEAS

- Balancing priorities
- Travel
- Handling Disappointments

OTHER TOPICS THAT CAN BE DISCUSSED

- Discipline
- Kindness
- Resiliency

WORDS TO KNOW

Students should provide "real world" definitions" and share with the class.

GROUP TALK

In small groups, have students work together to discover answers to the questions from the text and inject their opinion. Representatives from each group can share the answers from their groups with the class for a larger discussion.

RESEARCH MINUTE

Research ways for kids to deal with disappointments in their life. Make a list of them. Tell a friend the ones that you think are most effective and why.

JOURNAL

Explain what disappointments are, how they happen to everyone, and ways to deal with them.

Disappointments
pp. 153-170

| Balancing Priorities | Travel | Handling Disappointments |

Objective: I will not let disappointments cause me to quit.

| **Words to Know** | **"Handling Disappointments"** |

Based on the context of the reading for this lesson, create a "real world" definition for each of the following words with a partner. Write your definitions below.

▢ discipline

▢ disappointment

▢ overcome

▢ implications

GROUP TALK

Directions: Read the text and discuss the following questions in your group.

1. (pp. 153-154) How did Jaylan handle the disappointment of not being the mini-Grizz?

2. Why is it important to still be positive when things don't go your way?

3. What ways did Summer make Jaylan a priority as it deals with his birthdays?

4. Is it important to keep your family first, despite other difficulties that may arise at school or other places? Yes or No Explain.

√ **SEE WHAT YOU KNOW**   **LESSON 12**

1. What great opportunity allowed Jaylan the opportunity to be around NBA players while they played in a game?
    - A. **becoming a ball boy**
    - B. becoming min-Grizz
    - C. becoming a Grizzlies dancer
    - D. becoming an NBA player

2. (pp. 156-157) What experience did Jaylan have with the Grizzlies that his mom had when she was a teenager in high school?
    - A. He worked at a fast-food restaurant.
    - B. He instructed a cameraman.
    - C. He got to shoot a winning shot in the game.
    - D. **He was in a commercial.**

3. (p. 159) How did Summer balance her priorities to ensure she and Jaylan were able to fly to Washington, D.C.? (Use supporting details to support your answer.)
    Answers may vary. Summer began saving for their airline tickets months in advance, and they stayed at Chinitra's house when they arrived.
    Evidence: I prepared for the trip months in advance by saving to buy our airline tickets. Staying at Chinitra's house, we only needed money for our flights.

4. On the trip to Washington, D.C. that Summer took with her son, what were some of the places they visited? What do you think the trip did for her son?
    Answers may vary (opinionated). They visited the Lincoln Memorial, the Washington Monument, the Vietnam Veterans Memorial, and Smithsonian Museums. This exposed her son to historical sites helping him understand some things in school as well as things he had not heard in school. The trip made him excited about traveling and experiencing new places and seeing new things.

Summer's hard work continues to pay off when she completes the requirements for her MBA. With her new credentials, Summer realizes she has more options for her career and pursues a job with a higher salary and more normal work hours. After a period of avoiding relationships not wanting to end up hurting her son, Summer entertains the idea of bringing a man into their lives.

LESSON 13: "Dreaming"

OBJECTIVE

I will learn to face my fears and follow my dreams.

KEY IDEAS

- Having vision
- Hard Work
- Relationships

OTHER TOPICS THAT CAN BE DISCUSSED

- Mentoring
- Patience
- Endurance

WORDS TO KNOW

Students should provide "real world" definitions" and share with the class.

GROUP TALK

In small groups, have students work together to discover answers to the questions from the text and inject their opinion. Representatives from each group can share the answers from their groups with the class for a larger discussion.

RESEARCH MINUTE

Have students create a Vision Board by following the 5 steps on the link below. http://christinekane.com/how-to-make-a-vision-board/

JOURNAL

What do you think it will take for you to achieve your most desired dream? How can others help to make this happen?

Dreaming
pp. 171-186

Hard Work	Vision	Relationships

Objective: I will learn to face my fears and follow my dreams.

Words to Know

Based on the context of the reading for this lesson, create a "real world" definition for each of the following words with a partner. Write your definitions below.

- ☐ vision
- ☐ value
- ☐ unison
- ☐ rely
- ☐ relationship
- ☐ persevere

GROUP TALK

Directions: Read the text and discuss the following questions in your group.

1. What are some situations that show Summer displayed doubt in this text?

2. How do you normally respond when you feel like you shouldn't do something (have doubt)?

3. What does it mean to "defy the odds"? Name three of the visions/dreams that have come true for Summer demonstrating that she defied the odds?

4. What did Summer do to hold on to her dreams in spite of her early mistake?

√ **SEE WHAT YOU KNOW**   **LESSON 13**

1. "Smiling at Everett with <u>disbelief</u> and even slight disapproval, I said, "Oh, he shouldn't have done that, but that was nice. Tell him thank you."
   Based on the usage of the word, "disbelief," in the sentence above, which of the following is a synonym for the word?
   A. surprise
   B. happiness
   C. joy
   D. sadness

2. "Because I attended a satellite campus of the college, my graduation occurred in Jackson, Mississippi at the main campus of Belhaven College. "
   What does the author mean by a "satellite" campus?
   A. She went to the main campus of the college.
   B. She went to space to take the class.
   C. She attended college at a location separate from the main college campus.
   D. She attended college in Jackson, Mississippi.

3. (p. 173) What is the purpose of "Big Brothers/Big Sisters"?
   (Use supporting details to support your answer.)
   Answers may vary. The purpose of "Big Brothers/Big Sisters" is to give children in single parent homes a positive role model who spends time with them.
   Evidence: The list was full of little black boys in single mother homes with mothers like me, desperately seeking a male role model for their sons.

4. At this point in the text, which relationship was Summer doubtful and scared about?
   (Use supporting details to support your answer.)
   Answers may vary. Summer was scared and doubtful about being with Everett in a relationship.
   Evidence: I'm sorry, but I can't do that. You just don't understand how hurt he'll be when you decide to leave us alone."

The story closes with Summer reflecting on how she began her journey as a shy, bullied girl with low self-esteem that followed her through adolescence. By the end of the book, she was a confident and successful young mother who had overcome many obstacles and was starting a new journey with a new job and preparing for a new life as a wife. She had beat the statistics that teen mothers face and was proud of her accomplishments, proud of her son, and ready for her next chapter.

LESSON 14: "Achieving Your Goals"

OBJECTIVE

I will learn the importance of education and success.

KEY IDEAS

- Adaptability
- Success

OTHER TOPICS THAT CAN BE DISCUSSED

- Strength
- Independence
- Perseverance
- Career

WORDS TO KNOW

Students should provide "real world" definitions" and share with class.

GROUP TALK

In small groups, have students work together to discover answers to the questions from the text and inject their opinion. Representatives from each group can share the answers from their groups with the class for a larger discussion.

MAP IT OUT!

Students will use the "Characteristics of Success" web to analyze things that contributed to Summer's success. Tell the kids to feel free to add more bubbles if they see necessary.

Relate the characteristics that contribute to Summer's success to anyone's success, even now while they're in school.

RESEARCH MINUTE

Using a Word Processing application, have students create an interactive Story Map that displays the route to achieving success in their life by reaching their futuristic goal(s).
http://www.readwritethink.org/classroom-resources/student-interactives/story-30008.html

JOURNAL

Explain how you can succeed, despite your circumstances—achieving your dreams.

Achieving Your Goals
pp. 187-203

Adaptability

Success

Objective: I will learn the importance of education and success.

Words to Know

Based on the context of the reading for this lesson, create a "real world" definition for each of the following words with a partner. Write your definitions below.

☐ education _____

☐ career _____

☐ self-motivated _____

☐ success _____

GROUP TALK

Directions: Read the text and discuss the following questions in your group.

1. In "Lessons Learned" on page 190, Summer said that "Education gives you options." What does that mean?

   _____
   _____

2. What kind of options do you believe education allows that is different from *not* having one?

   _____
   _____

3. How can education lead to a successful life?

   _____
   _____

4. What are some ways you can learn to adjust to a difficult class?

   _____
   _____

"Characteristics of Success"

Directions: In the web below, plug in characteristics of Summer's success as seen in the book.

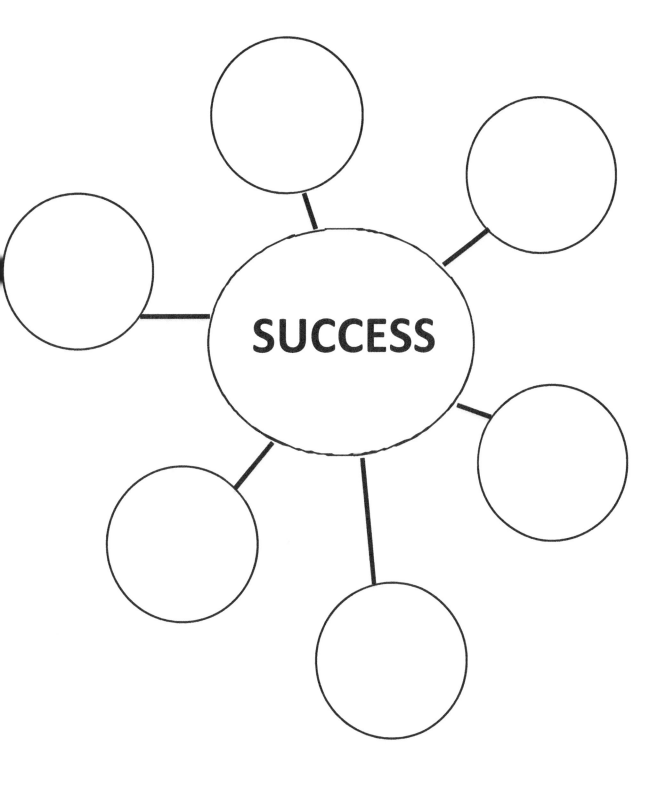

*Add more bubbles as needed.

The capstone project is a culminating activity that provides a way for you to demonstrate what you have learned over the course of engaging with this text and helps you to begin to discover your career path. Understanding who you are, what you want to be and do in the future, and what it takes to get there are crucial to your success. These factors guide your daily decisions both inside and outside of school. Investing your best effort in this project is purely for your benefit as it will be a key element to directing the choices you make from this point forward.

The capstone project includes three major elements.

1. The Paper
2. Career Shadow Figure
3. The Presentation

---

1. The Paper

Using the key ideas identified in each lesson, write an essay explaining why these are important for becoming a successful adult and being successful in a career you choose.

---

2. Career Shadow Figure

1) Using an empty 2-liter bottle, cover it with construction paper.
2) Choose a person who is working in or has worked a job you would like to do one day.
3) Print and cut out the facial image of that person.
4) Glue the facial image to the top of the bottle.
5) Create a list of the characteristics that describe that person and what he or she does for their career.
6) Cut out strips of words with those characteristics on it.
7) Glue the words on the cutout's image.

---

3. The Presentation

Present to the class in a 1-2 minute oral presentation of the information in the paper as well as the career shadow figure.

THE S.O. NOW WHAT? STATEMENT

At the end of this curriculum, have students write a "S.O. NOW what?" Statement identifying what they will do next in spite of that challenge. The point is to get students to think about situations in their lives or physical characteristics that they may or may not be able to change or do anything about. Often these are the very things that students are picked on about or that keep students from being able to learn or pursue success.

For example:

"S.O. What! I don't know my father."
"S.O. _NOW_ I will be a great father to my own children one day."

"S.O. What! I have a bucked teeth."
"S.O. _NOW_ I will embrace my features, get braces if I can afford them, and not make fun others because of their features."

"S.O. What! I don't have brand name clothes."
"S.O. _NOW_ I will focus on what's really important which is my education, and I will use my money wisely."

"S.O. What! I am short."
"S.O. _NOW_ I will embrace who I am and not make fun others because of their features."

"S.O. What! I have parents on drugs."
"S.O. _NOW_ I will not use drugs and encourage my friends not to do drugs either.

"S.O. What! I have a disability."
"S.O. _NOW_ I will focus on what I can do and not focus on what I cannot do."

Assess your classroom and the students' comfort levels to determine if it is appropriate to share these statements aloud. If the students are mature and willing to share, have the students express their next steps and encourage the class to support each student's challenges and efforts to improve their situations or feelings about themselves.

My S.O. *NOW* What? Statement

My name is

_____

and

So what I

_____

So *NOW* I

_____

www.SummerOwens.com

Made in the USA
Monee, IL
17 March 2022

93063344R00044